LIE DETECTOR
DETECTOR
Animals

WRITTEN BY
Kelly Milner Halls

ILLUSTRATED BY
Lee Cosgrove

PICTURE WINDOW BOOKS
a capstone imprint

Picture Window Books are published by
Capstone, 1710 Roe Crest Drive,
North Mankato, Minnesota 56003
www.capstonepub.com

© 2016 Weldon Owen
This edition by Picture Window Books,
a Capstone imprint.

Library of Congress
Cataloging-in-Publication Data
Cataloging-in-publication information is on file
with the Library of Congress.

ISBN 978-1-4795-8509-0 (hardcover)
ISBN 978-1-4795-8513-7 (paperback)
ISBN 978-1-4795-85175 (eBook PDF)

Written by Kelly Milner Halls

Printed in China
10 9 8 7 6 5 4 3 2 1

All photographs Shutterstock

LIE DETECTOR
DETECTOR
Animals

WRITTEN BY
Kelly Milner Halls

ILLUSTRATED BY
Lee Cosgrove

PICTURE WINDOW BOOKS
a capstone imprint

Can you tell the facts from the fibs and prove that you are the master of all things **animal?**

Animals are all around us. Some burrow into the soil to hide and help grass grow. Some animals soar through the air, while others swim through wavy waters. Some even curl up at our feet while we watch television!

How well do you know the animals that help to keep our world happy and healthy? Accept the challenge of the fact-or-fib questions to find out!

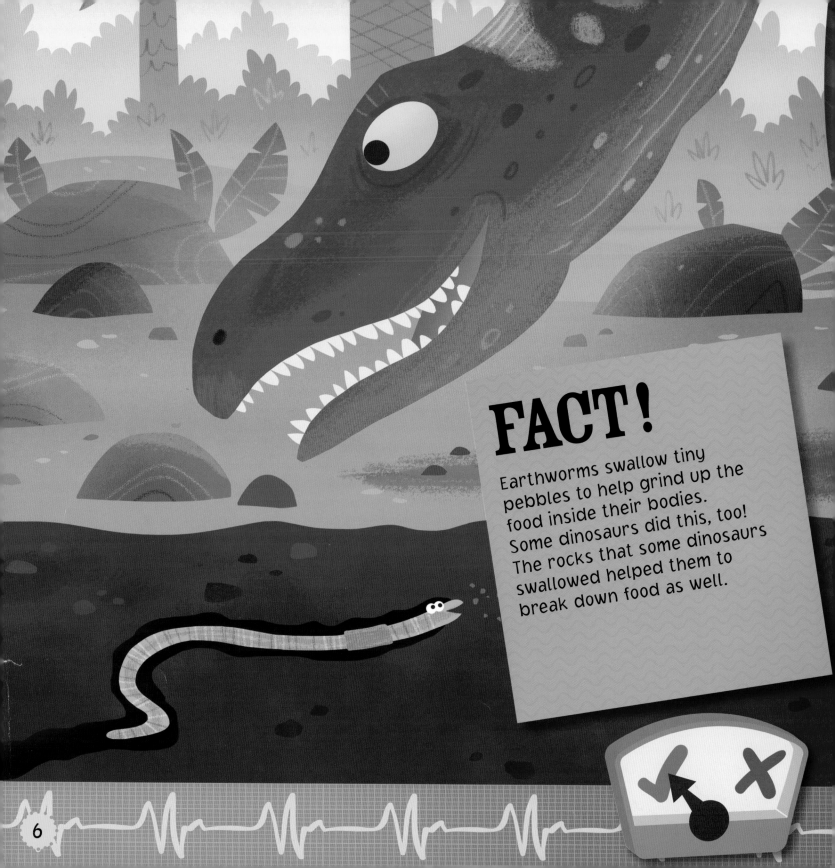

FACT!

Earthworms swallow tiny pebbles to help grind up the food inside their bodies. Some dinosaurs did this, too! The rocks that some dinosaurs swallowed helped them to break down food as well.

FIB!

Dragonflies are carnivores, or meat-eaters. They munch moths, flies, butterflies, and smaller dragonflies. But they can't bite people. Their mouths can't break human skin.

NO BONES ABOUT IT

Dragonflies may look like they have bones, but they don't. Like all insects, they are invertebrates. This means they have no backbone.

FACT!

Unlike fish, starfish have no brain and their blood is actually seawater! Scientists want to rename them sea stars because they are so different from fish.

FIB!

When two male king cobras fight, they can raise their bodies over 3 feet (1 meter) off the ground! They wrap their bodies around each other. Then each snake tries to pin the other to the ground. It looks like dancing, but it's really a lot more like arm wrestling!

Super Sleuth

Cobras are famous for the hood of skin at their neck. A cobra spreads its hood when it feels threatened or angry. The hood helps to scare away other animals.

FIB!

Some fish that live in the deepest parts of the ocean give off light. Their bodies create chemicals that make them glow. This is called Bioluminescence. But the light that they give off is not very bright.

Super sleuth

Fish are not the only animals with bioluminescence. Tiny fireflies light up the sky with their bioluminescent tails.

The **giraffe** is the world's tallest mammal, but its **legs** are surprisingly **short**.

FACT or FIB?

FIB!

A large part of a giraffe's impressive height comes from its long neck, of course. But giraffes also have very long legs. Each leg is nearly 6 feet (1.8 meters) long. That's taller than the average man! Six meerkats stacked on top of each other would be as tall as a giraffe's leg.

NOT A SLOWPOKE

Thanks to its long legs, a giraffe can walk at a speed of 10 miles (16 kilometers) per hour. That's about as fast as the average person jogs. For short bursts, a giraffe can run up to 35 miles (56 km) per hour!

Ouch! Hurry up!

FACT!

Chickens weigh too much to fly for more than a few seconds. The world record for chicken flight is just 13 seconds!. Still, these ground-dwelling birds can flap over fences that are less than 6 feet (1.8 meters) tall.

FACT!

Glands under a male gorilla's arms produce a strong, stinky scent. The smell sends a clear message to other gorillas to back off!

FIB!

Hippos spend most of their time soaking in water. When they do sunbathe, their skin makes a red, oily moisturizer. It acts as a natural sunscreen to keep the hippo's skin from burning.

Super sleuth

Hippopotamuses leave the water at sunset to graze on African grasses. On average, a hippo chomps 77 pounds (35 kilograms) of grass each night. That's the same weight as 1,400 small bags of potato chips!

23

FACT!

Scientists say that elephants are self-aware. This means that if they see their reflection, they know it's their own. Scientists think that only a few other animals are self-aware, including human beings, dolphins, chimps, and gorillas.

You called?

FACT!

There are more than 175 kinds of dogs. All of them are related to the gray wolf. About 25,000 years ago, humans started training wolves. Now dogs are our beloved pets.

FIB!

When the Texas horned lizard is being hunted, it stands very still, hoping to go unnoticed. If that doesn't work, the lizard puffs up to make itself look spiky.

Super Sleuth

Texas horned lizards are sunbathers. They spend their days lying in the sunlight. At night, they bury themselves in the sand. They are excellent diggers!

There's always more to discover!

We've only scratched the surface when it comes to animal facts. Scientists think that more than 8.7 million kinds of animals share the planet with us. And they find about 15,000 new species each year. It's exciting to think that new animal mysteries could be hiding right under your nose. So keep your eyes open and your notebooks ready! You never know what you are going to find!

Where to next?

TRACKER CHALLENGE

All animals have a different set of tracks. Just like human footprints, these are the shapes left behind in snow, mud, or sand. Tracks can be used to figure out which animals are living in an area. Do you have what it takes to match an animal to its tracks?

3. Which animal has the biggest footprint of them all?

1. Whose sharp-clawed paws are these?

2. Who uses their hands to climb trees?

4. Who uses their claws to scratch in the dirt for insects to eat?

5. Whose hooves are these?

6. Which animal has webbed toes that help it swim?

MATCH THE TRACKS TO THE ANIMALS BELOW:

A. Giraffe

B. Hippopotamus

C. Wolf

D. Elephant

E. Chicken

F. Gorilla

Answers: 1.C, 2.F, 3.D, 4.E, 5.A, 6.B

GLOSSARY

bioluminescence—the light that is made by some animals.

carnivore—an animal that eats only meat

gland—an organ in the body that makes natural chemicals or helps materials leave the body

invertebrate—an animal with no backbone

mammal—A warm-blooded animal that breathes air, has hair or fur and feeds milk to their young

moisturizer—a lotion that prevents something from drying out

species—a group of plants or animals wthat are the same

vertebrate—an animal with a backbone

INDEX